VICTORIA WIDE

Sensational Panoramic Views of Victoria

KEN DUNCAN

PANOGRAPHS®

12/19

Celebrated landscape photographer Ken Duncan was born in Mildura in far north-west Victoria, where the mighty Murray River sways across a semi-arid landscape made fertile by its languid waters.

From there, on the fringe of the Mallee's sparse scrubland, to Wilsons Promontory, the state's southernmost extremity, where elegant tree ferns crowd into rainforest gullies, the stunning diversity of Victoria makes it one of the most picturesque states in Australia. White turbulent ocean gives way to lush bush and carpets of green shagpile pasture; flat volcanic plains climb through rolling hills to become crags and bluffs; seasons slide together like the colours of the spectrum; and the past flows into the future with a continuity approaching gracefulness, born of the knowledge that this place is a treasure, an inheritance, a gift.

Returning to the state of his birth always rekindles Ken's love for its special magic, and his photographs capture its exuberant and haunting beauty.

TITLE PAGE
Brighton Beach Huts

THIS PAGE
Hopetoun Falls, Otway State Forest

When you're born on the Murray River, its changing waters leave an indelible mark on your soul. To me, the river is like a road that always leads me home.

It is a great pleasure to release this book in celebration of the opening of my new Melbourne Gallery. Home at last to share the beauty of God's creation in our great southern land.

This book is dedicated to the three most important people in my life - Jesus, Pamela and Jessica.

The new Ken Duncan Gallery is situated at:-
Shop U6 Southgate, Melbourne.
Telephone: (03) 9686 8022.

Proudly Sponsored by

FUJIFILM

The film Ken uses to capture the true colours of Australia

Craig's Hut, Alpine National Park

PREVIOUS PAGE
Tidal River Beach,
Wilsons Promontory National Park

THIS PAGE
Williamstown, Melbourne

NEXT PAGE
Aerial view of St Kilda

The Murray River, Victoria's northern boundary, slides away as inexorably as history. A century and more ago, magnificent paddlesteamers brought the vibrant energy of trade, commerce and entertainment to settlers along its banks, and fish from its waters found their way to the rich southern gold fields, where tens of thousands flirted with ruin to pursue gilded dreams.

Eventually the steamers fell silent, replaced by rail and road. Today a few surviving riverboats enable tourists to experience the hypnotic rhythm of the paddlewheel and the slow, melancholy glide of the river westward towards the sea.

PREVIOUS PAGE
Rolling Hills, Johanna

THIS PAGE
Paddlesteamers, Echuca Wharf

NEXT PAGE
Country garden, Mirranatwa, Serra Ranges

PREVIOUS PAGE
Croajingalong National Park

THIS PAGE
Sunset, Mansfield

PREVIOUS PAGE
Mackenzie Falls, Grampians National Park

THIS PAGE
North end, Refuge Cove, Wilsons Promontory

THIS PAGE
South end, Refuge Cove, Wilsons Promontory

NEXT PAGE
Melbourne City

The subtle pastel hues of morning rise over Melbourne's famous Flinders Street railway station. It is not yet rush hour, but the pulse of the city quickens in preparation for another hectic day. 'Under the clocks at Flinders Street' has long been one of the city's best-known meeting places. In the excitement of rapid change, will Melbournians still make time to meet friends 'under the clocks' as they did in the less frantic and perhaps more amiable past?

THIS PAGE
Flinders Street Station, Melbourne

NEXT PAGE
Mountain Ash, Strzelecki Ranges

PREVIOUS PAGE
The man from Snowy River, Mt. Buller

THIS PAGE
The Twelve Apostles at sunrise

THIS PAGE
The Twelve Apostles at sunset

NEXT PAGE
Wartook Reservoir, The Grampians

*I*n Victoria's southern rainforests, waterfalls drop like living curtains and stringy, jade-bright moss hangs from tree branches like candelabra. Tree ferns luxuriate in a glorious water-world of dew and rain and mist.

Victoria is eucalyptus country, with scrubby mallee gums standing around like mobs of kangaroos and rock-hard red gums lining rivers, the ancient watchmen of the land. Mountain ashes climb straight as sculpted columns eighty metres into the air while stringbarks cast off their lizard-skin in shreds on the ground. And up in the high country, great oceans of trees sweep away to every horizon, rising and falling across the folds of the earth, radiant reminders of joy.

PREVIOUS PAGE
Lake Mulwala, Yarrawonga

THIS PAGE
Triplet Falls, Otway State Forest

PREVIOUS PAGE
Freshwater Cove, Wilsons Promontory

THIS PAGE
Puffing Billy, The Dandenongs

NEXT PAGE
Quarry Beach, Mallacoota

PREVIOUS PAGE
Misty morning, Omeo Valley

THIS PAGE
The boys and their truck, Maldon

THIS PAGE
Maldon Primary School

NEXT PAGE
Majestic sunset, Mansfield

The rising sun, red as a campfire's glow in the bush mist, cracks the dawn open. Light ricochets off beach rocks, slides down city skyscrapers and catches twisted high country snow gums in vivid halos of gold.

There is subtlety about Victorian sunlight which the uninitiated can mistake for wanness. But locals appreciate the contrasting moods of nature's art - as intricate as the colours on a master painter's palette - illuminating landscapes with heaven's own light.

THIS PAGE
Morning light, Shipwreck Creek Inlet

NEXT PAGE
Broken Falls, Grampians National Park

PREVIOUS PAGE
Setting sun, Tidal River Beach

THIS PAGE
Coastal dunes, Thurra River

PREVIOUS PAGE
Pendergast Court, Benambra

THIS PAGE
Penders Cottage, Benambra

The Kelly brothers, Omeo Valley

The Twelve Apostles, Port Campbell

PREVIOUS PAGE
Snowy River gums,
Alpine National Park

THIS PAGE
Erskine Falls, Otway State Forest

NEXT PAGE
Murray River, Hattah-Kulkyne
National Park

The Arch, Great Ocean Road

VICTORIA WIDE
First published 1996
Reprinted 1999
Updated 2001
by Ken Duncan Panographs® Pty Limited
ABN 21 050 235 606
P.O. Box 3015, Wamberal NSW 2260, Australia.
Telephone: (02) 4367 6777.

The National Library of Australia
Cataloguing-in-Publication entry:
Duncan, Ken
Victoria wide: spectacular panoramic views
of Victoria.
ISBN 0 646 22695 9.
1. Victoria - Pictorial works. I. Title.
994.500222

To view the range of Ken Duncan's panoramic
Limited Edition Prints visit our Galleries situated at:-
- **Shop U6 Southgate, Melbourne, VIC, Australia.**
  Telephone: (03) 9686 8022.
- **73 George Street, The Rocks, Sydney, Australia.**
  Telephone: (02) 9241 3460.
- **5740 Oak Road, Matcham, NSW, Australia.**
  Telephone: (02) 4367 6701.